All Aboard

Passenger Trains

by Jenna Lee Gleisner

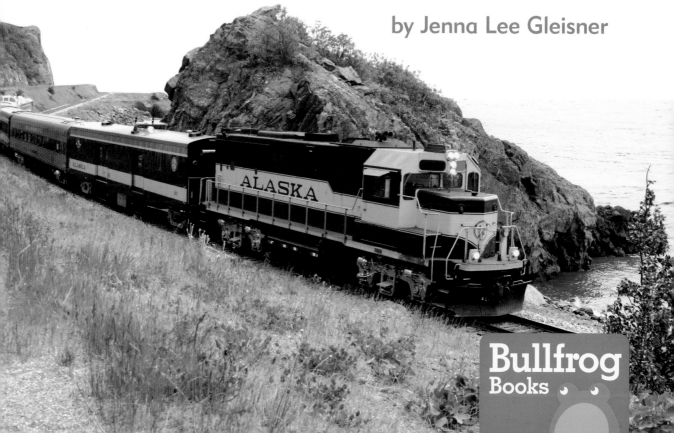

Bullfrog Books

Ideas for Parents and Teachers

Bullfrog Books let children practice reading informational text at the earliest reading levels. Repetition, familiar words, and photo labels support early readers.

Before Reading

- Discuss the cover photo. What does it tell them?

- Look at the picture glossary together. Read and discuss the words.

Read the Book

- "Walk" through the book and look at the photos. Let the child ask questions. Point out the photo labels.

- Read the book to the child, or have him or her read independently.

After Reading

- Prompt the child to think more. Ask: Have you ever ridden on a train, or would you like to?

Bullfrog Books are published by Jump!
5357 Penn Avenue South
Minneapolis, MN 55419
www.jumplibrary.com

Library of Congress Cataloging-in-Publication Data

Names: Gleisner, Jenna Lee, author.
Title: Passenger trains / by Jenna Lee Gleisner.
Description: Minneapolis: Jump!, Inc., 2020.
Series: All aboard
Includes bibliographical references and index.
Audience: Ages 5–8. | Audience: Grades K–1.
Identifiers: LCCN 2019022759 (print)
LCCN 2019022760 (ebook)
ISBN 9781645272465 (hardcover)
ISBN 9781645272472 (ebook)
Subjects: LCSH: Passenger trains—Juvenile literature.
 Railroads—Passenger traffic—Juvenile literature.
Classification: LCC TF148 .G5627 2020 (print)
LCC TF148 (ebook) | DDC 385/.22—dc23
LC record available at https://lccn.loc.gov/2019022759
LC ebook record available at https://lccn.loc.gov/2019022760

Editors: Jenna Trnka and Sally Hartfiel
Designer: Molly Ballanger

Photo Credits: Worldpics/Shutterstock, cover; Thomas Crosley/Shutterstock, 1; Steve Hiscock/Shutterstock, 3; Kaori Ando/Image Source/SuperStock, 4; Ben Cooper/SuperStock, 5; sturti/iStock, 6–7; Yuriy Chertok/Shutterstock, 8, 23tr; Julia Kuznetsova/Shutterstock, 9, 23bl; Caia Images/SuperStock, 10–11, 23tm; Uatp1/Dreamstime, 12–13 (train car); worldclassphoto/Shutterstock, 12–13 (window scene); Bernard Weil/Getty, 14–15; Ric Jacyno/Shutterstock, 16, 23br; Petr Podrouzek/Shutterstock, 17; miroslav _ 1/iStock, 18–19, 23bm; GODONG/BSIP/SuperStock, 20–21, 23tl; Pixel-Shot/Shutterstock, 24.

Printed in the United States of America at Corporate Graphics in North Mankato, Minnesota.

Table of Contents

Carrying Us

Let's take a ride!

Passenger trains carry us.

Where can we go?

All over!

Many of these trains
are in cities.

They take people
to work.

This train has
one locomotive.

It pulls coach cars.

coach
car

locomotive

We sit in a coach car.

9

conductor

ticket

10

A conductor works.

She takes our tickets.

Some trains
go a long way.

The trip is long.

There is a car
to sleep in.

sleeping car

13

dining car

There is a dining car.

We eat here.

Some trains carry tourists.

This one goes by the Grand Canyon!

steam ···▶

Some have a
steam locomotive.

Cool!

Where do you want to go?

All aboard!

Where in the United States?

Where can you take a trip on a passenger train in the United States? This map shows where Amtrak trains go.

- ● major city station
- — Amtrak route

Picture Glossary

aboard
On or onto a train, ship, or aircraft.

conductor
The person in charge of the train who takes tickets and keeps passengers safe.

locomotive
An engine used to push or pull railroad cars.

passenger
Someone besides the driver who travels in a vehicle.

steam locomotive
A locomotive that is powered by a steam engine.

tourists
People who are traveling for pleasure.

Index

To Learn More

Finding more information is as easy as 1, 2, 3.

❶ Go to www.factsurfer.com

❷ Enter "passengertrains" into the search box.

❸ Choose your book to see a list of websites.

FACT SURFER